85 Lesson Launchers

Basic Grammar and Usage

WALCH EDUCATION

SGS-SFI/COC-US09/5501

1   2   3   4   5   6   7   8   9   10
ISBN 978-0-8251-6338-8
Copyright © 2010
J. Weston Walch, Publisher
40 Walch Drive • Portland, ME 04103
www.walch.com

Printed in the United States of America

Introduction

Walch Education's *85 Lesson Launchers* series is a wonderful way to turn extra classroom minutes into valuable learning time. Use the 85 quick activities at the beginning of class to focus students on instruction; near the end of class to make good use of transitional time; in the middle of class to shift gears between lessons—or whenever you have minutes that now go unused. *85 Lesson Launchers* are a natural lead-in to more in-depth activities.

85 Lesson Launchers are easy to use. Simply photocopy the day's activity and distribute it. Or, make a transparency of the activity and project it on the board. Use the activities for extra credit points or to check your students' skills as they are acquired and built over time.

85 Lesson Launchers are a convenient and useful supplement to your regular class lessons. Make every minute count!

Find the Nouns

A **noun** is a word that names a person, a place, a thing, or an idea.

Examples:

| doctor **(person)** | beach **(place)** | apple **(thing)** | happiness **(idea)** |

Underline the nouns in the following sentences.

1. Lily jumped over the puddle.

2. Anthony likes to play hockey.

3. Mrs. Mason read a book to our class.

4. George Washington was our first president.

5. The United States is a nice place to live.

6. My dad bought me a new ball.

7. Casey was sad when she spilled her milk.

8. John reads the newspaper every day.

9. Sophie watches the stars at night.

10. Australia is a beautiful country.

A Proper Family Tree

A proper noun names a particular person, place, thing, or idea. Proper nouns are *always* capitalized.

Complete the family tree with names of the members of your family. You should include anyone who is important to you, such as parents, foster parents, brothers, sisters, and cousins. You may even write the names of your pets if you want!

85 Lesson Launchers: **Basic Grammar and Usage**
© 2010 Walch Education

Signed, Sealed, and Delivered!

A **proper noun** names a particular person, place, thing, or idea. Proper nouns are always capitalized.

Address the envelope below to a friend. Circle all of the proper nouns.

_____
Your name
_____
Your street
_____
Your town

USA   37¢

_____
Your friend's name
_____
Your friend's street
_____
Your friend's town

Now, write your friend a letter. Be sure to use at least five proper nouns in your letter. Circle all of the proper nouns.

_____
_____
_____
_____
_____
_____
_____
_____
_____
_____

A School of Nouns

A **collective noun** names a group or a unit.

Examples: team
flock

Circle the collective nouns.

person	Uncle Dennis	class
crew	team	coach
crowd	desk	Thomas Jefferson
committee	computer	group
family	pencil	assembly
army	troop	mouse
constellation	candle	doctor

85 Lesson Launchers: **Basic Grammar and Usage**
© **2010 Walch Education**

Which Noun Is Which?

Two different types of nouns are **common** and **collective.** Determine which noun is which. Place a circle around each common noun and a square around each collective noun.

Example: wolf **(common)**   pack **(collective)**

1. shampoo   flag   team

2. crowd   pen   colony

3. glass   hammer   pair

4. crew   species   paper clip

5. napkin   daisy   army

6. television   chorus   hat

7. committee   basket   camera

8. game   staff   ocean

9. club (of people) pack   pillow

10. marker   eraser   band

Make It Plural!

A **plural noun** names more than one person, place, thing, or idea. Usually, an **s** is added to a noun in order to make it plural. However, if a singular noun ends in **s, x, ch,** or **sh,** an es is added in order to make it plural.

Example: one **box**   two **boxes**

Write the plural form of the following nouns.

1. house _____   2. chick _____

3. fox _____   4. church _____

5. bush _____   6. class _____

7. bucket _____   8. couch _____

9. shirt _____   10. book _____

11. movie _____   12. bus _____

13. radish _____   14. rocket _____

15. beach _____   16. carrot _____

17. circus _____   18. toothbrush _____

19. shoe _____   20. porch _____

Where Does It Go?

Sort the following nouns. If the noun is singular, put it in the **Singular** column. If the noun is plural, put it in the **Plural** column. Then add three nouns of your own to each column.

pizza	student	pennies	flower
hats	person	clouds	houses
bees	rabbit	seagull	people
jacket	boots	turkey	fireflies

Singular

one apple

_____

_____

_____

_____

_____

_____

_____

_____

Plural

three apples

_____

_____

_____

_____

_____

_____

_____

_____

What Do They Possess?

Make the following nouns show possession. Add an apostrophe or an apostrophe and an **s** to the noun. Then write something on the line that the noun might possess. The first one has been done for you.

1. Keisha's sneakers _____

2. the teacher _____

3. Sally _____

4. the firefighter _____

5. the doctor _____

6. Mrs. Jones _____

7. the children _____

8. the cats _____

9. the team _____

10. the boy _____

11. Peter _____

12. the Smith family _____

13. Abraham Lincoln _____

14. Mr. Hess _____

15. the nurse _____

What's the Action?

A **verb** is a word that shows action. An action verb tells what something or someone does.

Examples: I **raised** my arms.
I **ran** past the finish line.
(Both of the bold words are **verbs.**)

Underline the verbs in the following sentences.

1. Betsy walked down the sidewalk.

2. Donna hit the tennis ball.

3. Mr. Madsen read the newspaper.

4. Mr. Watson pushed the grocery cart.

5. Catherine watched the soccer game.

6. The horse drank from the stream.

7. The monkey swung from the tree.

8. Mrs. Lin drove her car to the city.

9. Carla jumped into the pool.

10. Daphne picked the flowers.

Susie's Day

A **verb** tells what someone or something does. Some verbs show **action.**

      Examples: Rosa **ran** to the ball field.
                 Brian **caught** the ball.

Underline the action verbs in the following story.

What a Day!

One day, Susie woke up late. She rushed out of bed. Susie threw on her clothes and brushed her hair. She ran down the stairs to eat her breakfast. After breakfast, she brushed her teeth. She waved good-bye to her mother and hurried out the door. Susie saw the bus. The bus stopped in front of her house. Susie jumped on. She greeted her friends. The bus driver drove away. Susie began her school day.

---

85 Lesson Launchers: **Basic Grammar and Usage**
© 2010 Walch Education

What Are They Doing?

An **action verb** shows that an action is taking place.

Examples: Andy **paints** a picture.   Sasha **eats** pizza for lunch.

Read the sentences below. Find the action verb and write it on the line next to the sentence.

1. Jake walked to school. _____

2. Keyana rides her bike. _____

3. Ross swims in the lake. _____

4. Anthony jumped up from his desk. _____

5. The girls watched television. _____

6. The cat pounced on the mouse. _____

7. Josh scored a goal. _____

8. Mrs. Jones read the book to us. _____

9. Benjamin talks all the time. _____

10. The dog licked my face. _____

To Be or Not to Be?

Some verbs are **linking verbs.** A **linking verb** links a noun with some information about the noun. A common linking verb is the verb **to be.** The verb **to be** does not show action. It shows a **state of being.**

Singular	Plural
I **am**	we **are**
You **are**	you **are**
he/she/it **is**	they **are**

The following sentences have been started for you. Add the correct form of the verb **to be,** plus some information about the subject.

1. The name of my school _____

2. My teacher _____

3. The students in my class _____

4. Our principal _____

5. The playground _____

6. The cafeteria _____

7. The hallways _____

8. My classroom _____

9. My desk _____

10. My school _____

85 Lesson Launchers: **Basic Grammar and Usage**
© 2010 Walch Education

A Helping of Verbs

Some verbs **help** other verbs. **Helping verbs** never stand alone.

Example: Molly **must work** today.

In this sentence, the word **work** is the main verb. The main verb tells us the action of the sentence. The word **must** is the helping verb. It works together with the main verb.

Common Helping Verbs					
is	are	was	am	were	been
shall	will	would	did	must	can
may	have	had	has	do	should

Read the following sentences. Write the helping verb on the line.

1. You should see this spider! _____

2. Janet was sleeping when the phone rang. _____

3. Mason will sneeze if he gets near that cat. _____

4. Michael has seen that movie ten times! _____

5. You may walk to the store if you take Carl with you. _____

6. I shall read this chapter of the book. _____

Now, write two of your own sentences using helping verbs.

7. _____

8. _____

Past or Present?

Verbs in the **present tense** show what is happening now. Verbs in the **past tense** tell what has already happened.

Examples: I see the bird outside. **(present)**
I saw the bird outside. **(past)**

Read the following sentences. Underline the verb in each sentence. On the line beside each sentence, write whether the verb is **present** or **past** tense. The first sentence has been done for you.

1. Ms. Ito <u>reads</u> the book. <u>present</u> _____

2. Jamie sits quietly in his chair. _____

3. Susan sang the song beautifully. _____

4. Our neighbor's dog barks constantly. _____

5. Maria looks pretty in her new dress. _____

6. Yesterday Cory rode his bike to school. _____

7. The clouds float above us. _____

8. The bird flew by my window. _____

9. Sam laughed at Mr. Lloyd's joke. _____

10. I slept in my new bed last night. _____

11. Taylor swam the whole length of the pool. _____

12. Debbie plays in the backyard. _____

What Will Happen?

Present tense verbs tell us what is happening now. **Future tense verbs** tell us what **will** happen. Most verbs are changed to the future tense by adding **will in front of** the verb. If there is an **s** on the end of the verb, drop it when you make the verb into the future tense.

Examples: I **play** the flute in the school band. **(present)**
I **will play** the flute in the school band. **(future)**
Damien **plays** hockey. **(present)**
Damien **will play** hockey. **(future)**

Change the following verbs from present tense to future tense. Write the new sentence on the line.

1. The bird sings.

   _____

2. Jade colors in her coloring book.

   _____

3. John washes his new car.

   _____

4. Our cat meows.

   _____

5. I hit the tennis ball.

   _____

6. Derek sails in a little sailboat.

   _____

7. The dog eats his food.

   _____

8. Carrie swims in the swimming pool.

   _____

Irregular Verbs

Not all verbs can be changed to the past tense by adding a **d** or an **ed.** These verbs are called **irregular verbs.**

Examples: I **go** to the movies. **(present)**
I **went** to the movies. **(past)**

Draw a line from the present tense of the verb to the correct past tense. Use a dictionary, if needed.

Present	Past
1. see	swam
2. am	came
3. come	flew
4. eat	saw
5. freeze	rang
6. swim	chose
7. wear	was
8. ring	froze
9. shake	fought
10. fight	stole
11. choose	wore
12. fly	ate
13. steal	drank
14. write	shook
15. drink	wrote

Back to the Present

Read each of the following verbs under the space. Then change the past tense of the verb to the present tense. Write each new verb in the space.

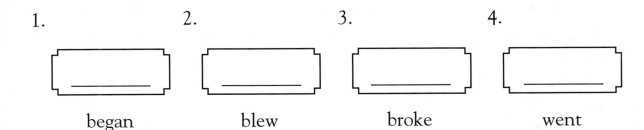

1. _____
   began

2. _____
   blew

3. _____
   broke

4. _____
   went

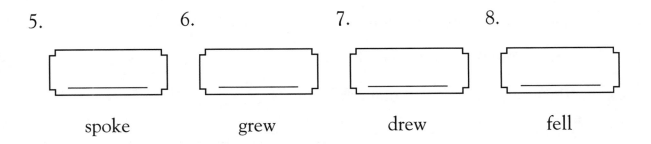

5. _____
   spoke

6. _____
   grew

7. _____
   drew

8. _____
   fell

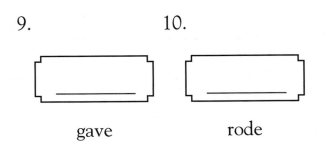

9. _____
   gave

10. _____
    rode

One, Two, Three, or More?

Verbs always agree *in number* with their subjects. If you have a **singular subject,** you must have a **singular verb.** If you have a **plural subject,** you must have a **plural verb.**

Examples: Our dog barks. **(singular)**   Our dogs bark. **(plural)**

Note the change in the verb when the *number* of the subject changes.

On the lines next to the sentences below, write if the verb in the sentence is singular or plural.

1. Our parents help us in the classroom. _____

2. The candle burns slowly. _____

3. We ride our bikes after school. _____

4. The kittens meow to get attention. _____

5. That flashlight is not very powerful. _____

6. Flowers bloom all summer long. _____

7. The bird sings softly in the tree. _____

8. Those clouds are very dark. _____

9. Trees line the driveway. _____

10. Sarah loves to go to the beach. _____

85 Lesson Launchers: **Basic Grammar and Usage**
© 2010 Walch Education

Make It Plural!

You know that some verbs are **singular** and some are **plural.** One easy way to make a singular verb into a plural verb is by dropping the **s** at the end of the verb.

Examples: Janie **reads** all the time.
(The singular form of the verb has an **s.**)
Students **read** all the time.
(The plural form does not have an **s.**)

Read the following sentences. Change each verb in **bold** letters from singular to plural. Write the plural form of the verb on the line.

1. Kate **plays** tennis every Thursday. _____

2. Paul **eats** hot dogs for lunch every day. _____

3. My cat **sleeps** on my bed. _____

4. Kim's bird **talks** to her! _____

5. Mr. Cobbett **writes** on the chalkboard during class. _____

6. Our dog **swims** in the lake. _____

7. Susie **walks** to school. _____

8. Thomas always **listens** during class. _____

9. That cake **looks** delicious! _____

10. My hair **grows** really fast. _____

Double Meanings

Some words can be used as a **noun** or as a **verb.**

Examples: I love to **fish** with my dad.
(In this sentence, **fish** is a verb.)
The **fish** are really jumping today!
(In this sentence, **fish** is a noun.)

Read the following sentences. Decide whether the word in **bold** letters is a noun or a verb. Write **noun** or **verb** on the line next to the sentence.

1. The **float** is out at the edge of the swim area. _____

2. Can you **float** in the water? _____

3. Don't **jump** into the shallow end of the pool! _____

4. That **jump** was not as high as I thought it was. _____

5. That **shovel** is perfect for digging at the beach. _____

6. Can you **shovel** that snow for us? _____

7. _Beauty and the Beast_ is Erin's favorite **play.** _____

8. Can you come out and **play** after school? _____

9. **Look** at all of the birds! _____

10. Don't give me that **look!** _____

85 Lesson Launchers: **Basic Grammar and Usage**
© 2010 Walch Education

Who Are You?

An **adjective** is a word that describes a noun.

What kind of person are you? What do you look like? Are you kind or funny? List six adjectives that describe you and write them on the lines.

1. I am _____

2. I am _____

3. I am _____

4. I am _____

5. I am _____

6. I am _____

An Indefinite Answer

An *article* is a type of adjective. **A, an,** and **the** are articles. **The** is a *definite article*. It describes a specific noun. **The** is used with both singular and plural nouns.

> **Example:** *The* dog barked at the strangers.

A and **an** are *indefinite articles*. They describe any one of a group of nouns. **A** and **an** are only used with singular nouns.

> **Examples:** *A* bird has wings.   *An* ostrich has wings, but it does not fly.

Write **a** or **an** on the lines.

1. the parrot   ⟶   _____ parrot

2. the house   ⟶   _____ house

3. the beach   ⟶   _____ beach

4. the umpire   ⟶   _____ umpire

5. the whale   ⟶   _____ whale

6. the ocean   ⟶   _____ ocean

7. the tractor   ⟶   _____ tractor

8. the envelope   ⟶   _____ envelope

9. the flashlight   ⟶   _____ flashlight

10. the infant   ⟶   _____ infant

85 Lesson Launchers: **Basic Grammar and Usage**
© 2010 Walch Education

Let's Go Skiing!

Remember, **articles** can be **definite** or **indefinite**. A **definite** article describes a specific noun. An **indefinite** article describes only one of a group of nouns.

> **Definite:** **the** horse, **the** tree, **the** child, **the** ant
> **Indefinite:** **a** horse, **a** tree, **a** child, **an** ant

Read the following story. Fill in each blank with the appropriate article.

A Day on the Slopes

Last December, Nick's family went skiing in Vail, Colorado. When they arrived at _____ ski area, Nick was very excited. He looked around at all of _____ people. They carried skis, poles, and snowboards. Nick had _____ brand-new pair of skis. He couldn't wait to try them! His sister, Kate, had _____ older snowboard that she had borrowed. She was eager to get on the slopes. Nick went into _____ lodge to put on his ski boots. He put on _____ heavy pair of socks. Then he put on his boots. After wrapping _____ scarf around his neck, he was ready to go! He went out into _____ cold and put on his skis. He and his father got in line at _____ chairlift. When _____ chair came around, Nick hopped on. _____ chairlift brought Nick and his father all _____ way to _____ top of _____ mountain. They got off of _____ chairlift and waited for Kate and Mom. When all four of them were at _____ top, they pulled down their goggles. Nick skiied down _____ mountain. It was _____ great day!

You Choose an Adverb!

An **adverb** describes a verb, an adjective, or another adverb. Adverbs tell *how, where, when,* and *how much.* Many adverbs end in **-ly.**

Examples: Walk **carefully** to your classroom.
The children worked **well** together.

Read the following sentences. Write an adverb on the line. Remember, your sentence needs to make sense!

1. Carolyn ran _____ down the street.

2. Tyson plays the piano _____.

3. The oak trees swayed _____ in the wind.

4. The sea crashed _____ on the shore.

5. Those clouds are moving _____.

6. The dog snored _____.

7. She swam _____ to the float.

8. The baby cried _____.

9. Don't hit it so _____.

10. The palm trees are _____ tall.

Adverbs Versus Adjectives

Read the following sentences. Write if the word in **bold** letters is an adjective or an adverb. Then, draw an arrow from the word in **bold** to the word that it describes or modifies. The first one has been done for you.

1. Don't talk so **loudly**. <u>adverb</u>

2. The bat flew **silently** above our heads. _____

3. Sarah plays the piano **really** well. _____

4. **The** play was very entertaining. _____

5. I walk **faster** if I wear my sneakers. _____

6. Shannon splashed **cold** water on her face. _____

7. Our school is located in a **really** old building. _____

8. **Some** people are allergic to bees. _____

9. Have you ever seen **an** octopus? _____

10. That grass is really **tall!** _____

11. The sea was **choppy** after the storm. _____

12. Do you like watching **scary** movies? _____

13. We whispered **very** quietly. _____

14. He is a really **good** baseball player. _____

15. Please don't squeeze my hand so **tightly.** _____

Substitute Pronouns

Pronouns replace nouns. Pronouns can refer to **people, places, things,** or **ideas.** Pronouns are often used so that we do not need to use the same noun over and over again.

we	them	he
they	she	it

Choose a pronoun from the box to replace the underlined noun in each sentence. Write the pronoun on the line. You will use some pronouns more than once.

1. The <u>duck</u> jumped into the river. _____

2. My <u>sister</u> and <u>I</u> went hiking last fall. _____

3. The <u>flowers</u> have been blooming for days. _____

4. <u>James</u> loves to play lacrosse. _____

5. <u>Martha</u> reads every day. _____

6. The <u>fish</u> are swimming by the rocks in the pond. _____

7. We rode our <u>bikes</u> to the desert. _____

8. All of the <u>houses</u> on our road are painted white. _____

9. The <u>birds</u> chirp loudly every morning. _____

10. Where is your <u>hat</u>? _____

85 Lesson Launchers: **Basic Grammar and Usage**
© 2010 Walch Education

Pronoun Possession

Pronouns replace nouns. Pronouns can refer to **people, places, things,** or **ideas.** Some pronouns show possession.

Example: Mike rode Mike's bike. ➤ Mike rode *his* bike.

Possessive Pronouns
my, mine, your, yours, his, her, its, our, their

Read the sentences below. Circle the correct pronoun.

1. (Our, Him) house is white with a black roof.

2. That baseball bat is (mine, it).

3. The kittens have (her, their) own little tree house.

4. Jane gave (her, their) sunglasses to Tomas when the sun came out.

5. The whole class loved (their, her) teacher.

6. Mary forgot the key to (yours, her) house.

7. That watch is (them, mine)!

8. We love (our, him) gerbil.

9. (Your, Mine) shirt is too big for you!

10. The players grabbed (their, your) baseball gloves before they ran onto the field.

11. Danny left (his, their) books at school.

12. The school was very proud of (him, its) students.

13. The cat licked (their, its) paws.

14. We have (our, their) own swimming pool.

15. Kevin went to see (his, its) uncle in New York.

Name That Conjunction!

A **conjunction** connects a word or group of words with another word or group of words. Some conjunctions are used in pairs.

Conjunction Pairs	
either, or	both, and
neither, nor	whether, or

Read the following sentences. Circle the conjunctions. The first one has been done for you.

1. (Neither) Jason (nor) Sue likes to watch television.

2. He was both the brightest student in the class and the nicest.

3. Would you please either quiet down, or stop talking?

4. I don't know whether I want to ski or snowboard.

5. Samantha is both sweet and talented.

6. Neither Jose nor Ralph is going to the park.

7. Whether Louis visits or not, we will go on a bike ride.

8. Both Jackie and I play basketball.

*85 Lesson Launchers: **Basic Grammar and Usage***
© 2010 Walch Education

Please Don't Interject!

An **interjection** is a word or group of words used to show strong feeling, emotion, or surprise. An interjection is usually followed by an exclamation point.

Read the following sentences. Circle the interjections. If the sentence does not contain an interjection, do not circle anything.

1. Wow! What a great magician.

2. Can you believe he did that? Jeepers!

3. Ouch! Please don't pinch me!

4. Did you see that?

5. Cool! Can you do that again?

6. Don't run on the pool deck! Oops!

7. Uh-oh! I forgot my swimsuit!

8. Help! I've got my hand stuck!

9. Gosh! I didn't realize that you were so smart!

10. Oh my goodness! That is the neatest thing I have ever seen!

11. Sweet! I wish I could do that!

12. Well, let's get going.

Test Your Noun Skills

Which words are common nouns? Which words are proper nouns? Place the words below into the columns marked **Common** and **Proper.**

London	computer	Abraham Lincoln
uncle	California	water

Common

_____

_____

_____

Proper

_____

_____

_____

Circle all of the collective nouns in the story.

The Wild Animal Park

On Tuesday, children from our school went to a wild animal park. The children on the soccer team went. The students from the school orchestra went. The boys and girls from the after-school club went. My family helped out on the trip, and they went, too. We saw a flock of birds. We saw a school of fish. We saw a pod of seals. We saw a herd of elephants and a pack of wolves. We even saw an army of ants at our picnic.

Change the following singular nouns into plural nouns.

1. penny _____
2. apple _____
3. beach _____
4. city _____

Add a pronoun to each sentence. Make sure each sentence makes sense.

5. We like _____.
6. Did you bring _____ bathing suit with you?
7. That is _____ favorite shirt.
8. They bought _____ plane tickets three months ago.

85 Lesson Launchers: Basic Grammar and Usage
© 2010 Walch Education

Show What You Know!

Circle all of the adjectives in the following story.

A Trip to the Zoo

I love to go to the zoo. My favorite animals are the giraffes. They are so neat with their long, skinny necks and their spots. I think it would be really cool to be able to reach my head way up into trees the way giraffes can. I also love the polar bears. They are so big and furry. I wonder if they are as soft and cuddly as they look!

Read the following sentences. Determine whether the word in **bold** letters is an adjective or an adverb. Then write **adjective** or **adverb** on the line.

1. Would you like to own **an** octopus? _____
2. That tree is **really** tall. _____
3. Are those pants **blue** or gray? _____
4. The **cold** water was very refreshing. _____
5. I am very **tired.** _____
6. Would you please walk **slower?** _____
7. **The** treehouse is my favorite place to go. _____
8. The candle burned **brightly.** _____

Write two interjections and two conjunctions on the following lines.

Conjunctions

_____

_____

Interjections

_____

_____

Write an adjective before each noun below.

9. _____ ocean
10. _____ fish
11. _____ clouds

Luck o' the Irish

The first letter of the first word in every sentence should always be **capitalized**. Lots of other words need to be capitalized, too! We capitalize months, days of the week, and holidays. We also capitalize the names of particular places and people. We capitalize the names of pets, too!

Read the following story. Circle the words in the story that should be capitalized and write the capital letters above them. If a word is capitalized and it shouldn't be, cross it out and write the lowercase letter above it.

A Green Day!

Every march my family gathers together. because we are a large irish family, March 17 is a very special Day for us. why? it is special because march 17 is st. patrick's day! our family dresses in green Clothing and dances to Irish music. my little cousin, bridget, performs irish step dancing for us. my aunt colleen makes Corned Beef and cabbage. my mother even makes green mashed potatoes! My uncle Reilly makes irish soda bread, an irish tradition. someday I hope to go to ireland and celebrate st. patrick's day there!

Holidays Around the Year

The names of days, months, and holidays are always **capitalized.**

Write the names of the months in the first column. Then write the name of a holiday that occurs in each month in the second column. Which month has no holiday? Write **no holiday** on that line.

Months   Holidays

1. _____   _____
2. _____   _____
3. _____   _____
4. _____   _____
5. _____   _____
6. _____   _____
7. _____   _____
8. _____   _____
9. _____   _____
10. _____   _____
11. _____   _____
12. _____   _____

Where in the World?

The names of cities, towns, and countries are always **capitalized.** Below is a list of cities and towns. Write the name of the state in which each city and town is located.

If it is a foreign city, write the name of the country. If you have difficulty, ask your teacher for help, or look on a map. Don't forget to capitalize!

City/Town	State/Country
1. London	_____
2. St. Louis	_____
3. Denver	_____
4. Los Angeles	_____
5. Paris	_____
6. Seattle	_____
7. Madrid	_____
8. Honolulu	_____
9. Toronto	_____
10. San Antonio	_____
11. Salt Lake City	_____
12. Baltimore	_____

Let's Talk About You

Names of particular people and places need to be **capitalized.** Answer the following questions. Don't forget to capitalize your answers when necessary.

1. Where do you live? _____

   _____

2. What is the name of one family member? _____

   _____

3. What is the name of a favorite pet? _____

   _____

4. What are the names of your three favorite cities? _____

   _____

5. Who is your favorite actor? _____

   _____

6. What is the name of a favorite storybook character? _____

   _____

7. What is the name of a favorite relative? _____

   _____

8. Where does this relative live? _____

   _____

A Capital Letter

Read the letter below. Circle the letters that should be **capitalized.** Remember, names of particular people, places, holidays, months, and days all need to be capitalized.

423 palm street
Sanibel island, florida 95860
august 22, 2003

Ms. gail Scott
2986 walker boulevard
Suite 46
Littleton, colorado 80128

Dear ms. Scott,

thank you for your interest in my puppies. I have been caring for golden retrievers since may of 1998. The puppies will be available in december, so you will have your puppy in time for christmas. I am happy to reserve one of rusty's puppies for you.

will you be flying from littleton to sanibel island? It would be best if you could fly into the fort myers airport. Arriving on a monday or thursday would be best. Could you let me know your plans by september 30?

i will look forward to hearing from you soon.

sincerely,

Pauline Roy

pauline roy

Capital Review

The first word in a sentence is always capitalized. The names of days, months, holidays, and the names of people, pets, and places are also capitalized.

Choose one of your favorite holidays. Write five sentences about the holiday. Why do you like it? Who do you visit on this holiday? When and why is it celebrated? What makes this holiday one of your favorites? Be sure to capitalize when necessary.

_____

_____

_____

_____

_____

_____

_____

Now, circle all of the words below that should be capitalized. If a word is capitalized and it should not be, cross out the capital letter.

new york	mount rainier	yellowstone national park
Water	alligator	wal-Mart
Rocks	wedding	statue of liberty
wednesday	december	independence day
labor day	Puppy	february
arkansas	book	monday
amsterdam	Refrigerator	video game

Period Practice Makes Perfect!

Periods have many uses. Not only do they come at the ends of sentences, but they are also used with **abbreviations.**

We use abbreviations all the time.

Examples: **Doctor** Sampson = **Dr.** Sampson

John **Fitzgerald** Kennedy = John **F.** Kennedy

Main **Street** = Main St.

If the abbreviation comes at the end of the sentence, only use one period.

Draw a line from each word on the left to its abbreviation on the right.

1. Mister   100 ft.

2. United States   F.D.R.

3. Reverend   Richard, Jr.

4. Kelly Colleen   Mr.

5. Park Avenue   Mon.

6. 100 feet   U.S.

7. Franklin Delano Roosevelt   Dec.

8. Monday   K.C.

9. December   Rev.

10. Richard, Junior   Park Ave.

Excuse Me, Mr. President

When a sentence asks a question, it must have a **question mark** at the end.

Imagine that you are going to visit the White House to meet the President. You can ask the President any questions that you want. Write eight questions that you would ask. Don't forget to put a question mark at the end of each question!

1. _____

2. _____

3. _____

4. _____

5. _____

6. _____

7. _____

8. _____

Choose the Punctuation

If a sentence is a **statement,** write a period at the end. **(.)**

If a sentence asks a **question,** write a question mark at the end. **(?)**

If a sentence **shows** a lot of **feeling** or **emotion,** write an exclamation point at the end. **(!)**

Write three sentences for each end mark. Examples have been done for you.

Periods

1. Summer is my favorite time of year. _____

2. _____

3. _____

4. _____

Question marks

5. Do you like summer better than winter? _____

6. _____

7. _____

8. _____

Exclamation points

9. That is the best summer vacation I have ever had! _____

10. _____

11. _____

12. _____

85 Lesson Launchers: **Basic Grammar and Usage**
© 2010 Walch Education

A Letter to Grandma

Read the following letter from Abby to her grandmother. Help Abby with end punctuation. In the answer boxes, place a period, question mark, or exclamation point to complete each sentence.

Dear Grandma,

How are you ☐ I am doing really well ☐

Next week is my last week of school ☐ I am so excited ☐

Mom and Dad have lots of fun things planned for the summer ☐ We are going to a water park and to the zoo ☐ I can't wait to see all of the animals ☐ Mom even said that I can bring a friend with me ☐

Are you going to come and visit soon ☐ I hope so ☐ I really miss you so much and can't wait to see you ☐

Lots of love,
Abby

It All Ends Here

Place the correct punctuation in the answer box at the end of each sentence.

1. My school has 400 students ☐

2. How many students go to your school ☐

3. Do you like music ☐

4. My teacher is great ☐

5. Ouch! That hurt ☐

6. Are you okay ☐

7. My mom works in a hospital ☐

8. Do you have a brother or a sister ☐

9. That's wonderful ☐

10. Do you want to visit our school ☐

85 Lesson Launchers: **Basic Grammar and Usage**
© 2010 Walch Education

Using Commas

Commas are used to make ideas in a sentence clear. Sometimes commas are used to separate words in a **series.**

Examples: This book is about **dogs, cats,** and **birds.**
There were **blue, pink,** and **yellow** candles on the cake.
Jack, Toni, and **Mitchell** went to the movies.

Write a sentence about each of the words in **bold** letters. Use the three words under each of the **bold** words in the sentence. Remember to use commas in a series.

Cloud
big
white
fluffy

_____

_____

_____

Tree
tall
green
pretty

_____

_____

_____

Flower
yellow
short
smooth

_____

_____

_____

When I Grow Up . . .

When a sentence begins with **Yes, No,** or **Well,** a comma follows the word.

Examples: **Yes,** I play baseball.
No, I am not a professional baseball player.
Well, let's find out who is!

Answer the following questions about what you want to do when you grow up. Begin each of your responses with **yes, no,** or **well.**

1. When you grow up, what kind of job would you like to have?

_____

2. Would your job be indoors?

_____

3. Would you work on a farm?

_____

4. Would you have your own office?

_____

5. Would you take a bus to your job?

_____

6. Would you be the boss where you work?

_____

7. Would you have fun at your job?

_____

Comma Madness

When you are addressing someone directly in a sentence, use a comma after his or her name.

     Example: Megan, you look very nice today.

When the person's name comes in the middle of the sentence, use a comma before and after the person's name.

     Example: I don't understand, Megan, why you wore pants on such a hot day!

Read each sentence below. Add commas where they are needed. Make a check (✔) next to sentences that are written correctly.

1. Please Veronica don't walk in the mud!

2. Aaron looks very sad today.

3. Emily why don't you come to the movies with us?

4. Mr. Moore may I go to the library?

5. Pete Sampras is a great tennis player.

6. George Washington was our first president.

7. Mom may I go out and play?

8. How do you get to Hawaii Uncle Harry?

9. I wonder Mrs. Mowatt if I can take that book home with me.

10. Jamie let's go swimming!

Set It Off!

An **appositive** is a word or group of words that explains or renames a noun or pronoun. Appositives are set off by commas.

> **Example:** Dr. Harpell, **my pediatrician,** is a great lady.
> (**My pediatrician** is an appositive. It tells us more about Dr. Harpell.)

Below is a list of nouns and a list of appositives. Write a sentence for each noun. Use the appositive in your sentence. Don't forget to use commas to set off the appositive.

Noun	Appositive
Juan	the team captain
Renee	my cousin from California
Tweety	my canary
The Hasans	the family that lives next door
Ms. Richards	the school librarian
Danielle and Frank	my aunt and uncle

1. _____

2. _____

3. _____

4. _____

5. _____

6. _____

Red Letter Days

Use a **comma** to separate the day and the year when you write a date. If the date comes in the middle of the sentence, use a comma after the year, too.

> **Examples:** We traveled to New York City on February 15, 2002.
> On June 13, 2001, my sister was born.

Add commas to the following sentences.

1. On November 3 1998 we got our first snow of the year.

2. We adopted our cat on March 26 1995.

3. On May 6 2001 my family went to our family reunion.

4. My cousin was born on October 17 2003.

5. July 4 2000 was a great Independence Day!

6. On December 23 2001 we had a huge snowstorm!

7. Aisha's sister was born on January 1 2003 New Year's Day!

8. On October 3 1997 Karen and Paul got married.

Write two sentences below that contain dates.

9. _____

_____

10. _____

_____

Around the World

A **comma** is used to separate a city from a state. It is used to separate a city from a country, too.

> **Examples:** My sister lives in Burlington, Vermont.
> My cousin traveled to Tokyo, Japan.

Add commas to the following sentences.

1. Julia lives in San Francisco California.

2. Big Ben is in London England.

3. Paul's aunt visits us in Boulder Colorado every summer.

4. Our family vacations in Bar Harbor Maine.

5. The Grand Tetons are in Jackson Wyoming.

6. The cruise ship stopped at Cancun Mexico.

7. I love to visit Montreal Canada.

8. My brother lives in Portland Oregon.

9. Every year we go skiing in Vail Colorado.

10. Mardi Gras is very exciting in New Orleans Louisiana.

85 Lesson Launchers: **Basic Grammar and Usage**
© 2010 Walch Education

Where Have You Been?

Have you ever traveled? Maybe it was only to another town in the state in which you live. Maybe it was to another state, or even to another country. Write the names of six places that you have visited. Be sure to write the city or town and state, or the city and country.

_____   _____

_____   _____

_____   _____

Now, write five sentences about the places that you have visited. Be sure to separate the city or town and state, or the city and country, with a **comma.**

1. _____

2. _____

3. _____

4. _____

5. _____

Compound Commas

A **compound sentence** has two independent clauses. An **independent clause** can stand alone as a sentence. Sometimes two independent clauses are joined together with a **conjunction.**

Examples: Winnie asked to watch television. Her mother said no.
Winnie asked to watch television**, but** her mother said no.
(When these two independent clauses are joined with a conjunction, such as **but,** a comma is placed between the two clauses.)

> ### Common Conjunctions
> and, but, or, nor, for, if, yet, so, because

Read the following sentences. All of the sentences are compound. Add a comma to the correct place in each sentence.

1. You said you wanted to go ice-skating yet you don't know how to skate!

2. My mother reminds me to wear a helmet but I always remember anyway.

3. I asked him to a movie and he said that he would go.

4. Do you want to go swimming or would you rather build a sand castle?

5. Mrs. Johnson said I could pick the flowers but they had already died.

6. The mall was closed so we went out to dinner instead.

7. Lily asked for a video game and her dad said she could get one.

8. I'd like you to go with us but you said that you were not interested.

Comma Camp

Brian is away at camp and has written a letter home about his camp adventures. Read the letter and add commas where they are necessary.

Dear Mom and Dad,

How are you? I am doing really well. I love being at camp. There are so many fun activities to do. My favorites are sailing soccer and pottery class. I am becoming a very good sailor! Dad wait until you see how much I know about sailing! I really like it. Soccer is also lots of fun. My counselor took us to a professional soccer game last Friday. We drove to Manchester New Hampshire and watched the game in a big stadium. It was really cool! I am also enjoying pottery. Can you believe it? Yes I am actually quite good! Mom I made you a really neat bowl. I can't wait to give it to you. The kids in my cabin are really nice, too. Michael the youngest one of us is also from Boston. He lives close to where we live.

Well I should get going. It is almost time for dinner. I hope you are doing well. See you soon!

Love
Brian

My Prized Possessions

A **possessive noun** is one that shows ownership. If you want to form the possesive of a singular noun, add an **apostrophe** and an s.

Examples: Robert's ruler
Tess's dress
Mary and Andrea's puppy

Read the nouns and the objects they possess below.

Nouns	Objects
1. Bill	book
2. the boy	shoe
3. Mom	car
4. Amy	baseball glove
5. Julia and Michelle	sister
6. the teacher	watch

Now, write sentences using each noun and object. In order to show that the noun **possesses the object,** add an **apostrophe** and an **s** to the correct noun. The first one has been done for you.

1. Bill's book was found on the bus. _____

2. _____

3. _____

4. _____

5. _____

6. _____

What Do They Possess?

Remember: If the **noun** is **singular,** add an apostrophe and an s to make the noun possessive.

If it is a **collective noun,** add an apostrophe and an s.

If the **noun** is **plural,** add an apostrophe and an s.

If the **noun** is **plural** and ends in an **s,** add an apostrophe only.

Read the following sentences. Add an **apostrophe** or an **apostrophe** and an **s** to each appropriate noun to show possession.

1. John baseball glove is old and worn out.

2. The boats masts are very tall.

3. The house shutters are painted green.

4. The team banner is brand-new.

5. A sunflower petals are yellow.

6. The roller coaster track was really curvy.

7. Vermont "claim to fame" is Ben and Jerry's ice cream.

8. The swans necks are very graceful.

9. The group colors are green and gold.

10. Jess scarf was pink and white.

Contraction Action

A **contraction** is written above each space below. On the line below the space, write the two words that make up the contraction.

1. you're

_____

2. he's

_____

3. we're

_____

4. it's

_____

5. didn't

_____

6. you'll

_____

7. couldn't

_____

8. he'll

_____

9. we'll

_____

10. they're

_____

*85 Lesson Launchers: **Basic Grammar and Usage***
© 2010 Walch Education

Don't Quote Me!

Quotation marks enclose the exact words of the speaker.

> **Examples:** "I love pizza," said Anthony.
> (Note: The comma comes *after* the
> spoken words, but *inside* the end
> quotation marks in the first sentence.)
> Josh said, "Pizza is my favorite, too."
> (The first letter of the first word of a quotation is
> capitalized. The comma comes after the word said.)

Read the following sentences. Tell whether the punctuation in the quotation has been written correctly. If it is correct, make a check (✔) on the line. If it is not correct, make an **X** on the line and make the needed change in the sentence. The first two have been done for you.

1. "Hi," said Jamie as she opened the door. ____✔____

2. Her mom answered, "ᴴᵒw was your day?" ____X____

3. Great! We had a spelling bee and I won Jamie replied _____

4. "You did? That is great said her mom. _____

5. Jamie said, "I got a blue ribbon for winning." _____

6. Let's put it on the refrigerator, said her mom. _____

7. Then her mom said, "we'll show Dad when he gets home." _____

8. "Then we will both be so proud of you," said her mom. _____

9. Jamie said "thanks, Mom." _____

10. In a shy voice, Jamie said, "I am proud, too!" _____

Quotation Marks or Underline?

Quotation marks are used to show titles of short stories, poems, and reports.

Example: "Sick" is my favorite Shel Silverstein poem.

Titles of books, magazines, movies, plays, and newspapers are **underlined.**

Example: <u>Harry Potter and the Sorcerer's Stone</u> is Jeffrey's favorite book.

Read the following titles. Put them in quotation marks or underline them.

1. Highlights Magazine
   (magazine)

2. Where the Sidewalk Ends
   (book)

3. The Rescuers Down Under
   (movie)

4. The New York Times
   (newspaper)

5. Finding Nemo
   (movie)

6. Amelia Earhart
   (report)

7. Sports Illustrated for Kids
   (magazine)

8. Two Friends
   (short story)

9. Lewis and Clark
   (play)

10. Animal Crackers
    (poem)

11. The Swing
    (poem)

12. Aro the Crow
    (short story)

Explaining Parentheses

Parentheses are used when a word or group of words is inserted into a sentence. This word or group of words is usually used to explain something in the sentence.

Examples: The U.N. (United Nations) helps people around the world. Our teacher is the best teacher in the whole school (everyone thinks so)!

Write four sentences. Use parentheses in each sentence.

1. _____

_____

2. _____

_____

3. _____

_____

4. _____

_____

Choose Your Parentheses!

Read the nouns and the information about each below.

1. My doctor   who works at the hospital

2. Denise   the youngest in her family

3. George   the smartest boy in our class

4. Mr. Peterson   my mother's nephew

5. The librarian   who used to be a teacher

6. My father   a college professor

7. My cousin   a firefighter

8. Mrs. Barnas   my teacher

Now, write a sentence about each noun and put the extra information in parentheses. The first one has been done for you.

1. <u>My doctor (who works at the hospital) is friendly to patients.</u>

2. _____

3. _____

4. _____

5. _____

6. _____

7. _____

8. _____

Subject Search

Every sentence has a subject. A **subject** tells who or what the sentence is about.

Read the following sentences. Write the subject on the line.

1. My aunt drinks tea every afternoon. _____

2. The cat tried to jump out of the cage. _____

3. The pavement gets really hot in the summer. _____

4. Our old umbrella broke in the gusty wind. _____

5. The phone at our house is always ringing! _____

Now, write five sentences of your own. Then circle the subject of each sentence.

6. _____

7. _____

8. _____

9. _____

10. _____

Insert a Subject

Every sentence has a subject. A **subject** tells **who** or **what** the sentence is about.

Example: Sometimes a **rainbow** appears after it rains.
(**Rainbow** is the subject of the sentence.)

Write a subject on the line to complete each of the following sentences.

1. A _____ lives in the water.

2. A _____ has four legs and two ears.

3. _____ has warm weather most of the year.

4. _____ fly in the sky.

5. _____ are comfortable to sit in.

6. A _____ keeps the rain off your head.

7. _____ is my favorite color.

8. _____ are my favorite animals.

9. _____ is a loud noise that you hear during thunderstorms.

10. _____ bark when they are excited.

85 Lesson Launchers: **Basic Grammar and Usage**
© 2010 Walch Education

Perfect Predicates

Every sentence has a **subject.** Every sentence also has a **predicate.** A **predicate** tells us more about the subject. The predicate tells us what the subject is, has, or does.

Example: Katie loves the color blue. (The **subject** of the sentence is **Katie.** The **predicate** of the sentence is **loves the color blue;** it tells us more about Katie.)

Underline the predicate in each of the following sentences. Remember, the predicate tells you more about the subject. One way to find the predicate is to ask yourself what the subject **is, has,** or **does.**

1. The fish has blue and green stripes.

2. The flowers are very pretty.

3. Akira went skiing last winter.

4. Matthew plays hockey every Monday night.

5. Fiona is the best pitcher on our softball team.

6. All the leaves fell off the tree.

7. Danny rode his bike to the boardwalk.

8. The house has green shutters.

9. The beach is covered with pretty seashells.

10. Disney World is home to Mickey and Minnie Mouse.

Who Is Your Hero?

Everybody has a hero. A hero is someone you look up to. A hero is someone who you want to be like. Think about who your hero is. What makes that person a hero to you? Write five sentences that describe your hero. Then underline the complete predicates in each of your sentences.

Example: My mom <u>is my hero</u>. She <u>is a great person</u>. She <u>is very caring</u>. My mom <u>is nice to everyone</u>. My mom <u>really cares about her family</u>.

1. _____

   _____

2. _____

   _____

3. _____

   _____

4. _____

   _____

5. _____

   _____

85 Lesson Launchers: **Basic Grammar and Usage**
© 2010 Walch Education

Add a Complement

A **predicate** always has a verb. Often, it has more than a verb. The part of the predicate that adds to the verb is called the **complement.**

On the left below are subjects. On the right are predicates. Draw lines to match each subject with a predicate that makes sense. Then underline the complement. Be sure to write the correct end mark in each box.

Subjects	Predicates
1. The rabbit	loves to eat watermelon.
2. Johnny	dribble the ball really well.
3. Mr. Ramirez	cried when she woke up.
4. The turtle	hopped through our backyard.
5. Bugs	plays on the lacrosse team.
6. My sister, Kristin,	is a great place to sail a boat.
7. The baby	watches the news every night.
8. The table	don't belong in the house.
9. The basketball players	has four legs.
10. The lake	is slower than the rabbit.

Finding the Right Complement

Every sentence has a subject and a predicate. Every predicate has a verb. A predicate usually has more than just a verb. It also has a **complement**. A **complement** is a word or group of words that completes the predicate.

Below are a list of subjects and verbs on the left and a list of complements on the right. Draw lines matching the subjects and verbs to the complements that fit. Then, write the sentences below.

Subject and Verb	Complement
The crowd yelled	very tired
The pilot flew	when the player scored
The sprinkler helps	my favorite meal of the day
Stuart looked	to Chicago every week
The castle was made	to water the garden
Breakfast is	entirely of stone

1. _____

2. _____

3. _____

4. _____

5. _____

6. _____

85 Lesson Launchers: **Basic Grammar and Usage**
© 2010 Walch Education

Subject and Predicate Review

Circle the simple subject in each sentence below.

1. The dictionary is a very useful tool.
2. Lemonade is my favorite summer drink.
3. Mrs. Knowles is our school librarian.
4. The Boston Celtics play at the Fleet Center.
5. I want to visit my grandmother in Phoenix.

Add predicates and end marks to the following subjects.

6. The geese _____
7. Theodore _____
8. Dr. Wells _____
9. Ants _____
10. The hawk _____

Write a subject on each line below.

11. _____ grow quickly if they are watered.
12. The _____ did their arithmetic after reading class.
13. _____ live in the ocean.
14. _____ is my favorite time of year.
15. _____ borrowed my bike yesterday.

Underline the complement in each of the following sentences.

16. You eat more slowly than I do!
17. Our horse lives in a barn behind our house.
18. The car began to smoke.
19. Thunderstorms are scary.
20. My dentist is really nice.

Hawaiian Agreement

The subject and verb in a sentence have to **agree** in number.

Examples: She is very tired. (The subject **she** is singular. Therefore, the verb **is** must be singular.)

The children sleep. (The subject **children** is plural. Therefore, the verb **sleep** must be plural.)

Circle the correct form of the verb in each of the following sentences.

1. Hawaii (is, are) a nice place to visit.

2. The islands (is, are) very beautiful.

3. Maui (has, have) many white, sandy beaches.

4. Maui (has, have) a beach with black sand.

5. Most beaches (has, have) white sand.

6. Sally (pick, picks) up seashells.

7. You can (look, looks) in the water, and you can (see, sees) lots of fish.

8. Marty (see, sees) a stingray!

9. Stingrays (is, are) not as scary as their name sounds.

10. Don't (hurt, hurts) them, and they won't (hurt, hurts) you!

85 Lesson Launchers: **Basic Grammar and Usage**
© 2010 Walch Education

Don't You Agree?

The subject and verb of a sentence must **agree.** If the subject is singular, then the verb must be singular. If the subject is plural, then the verb must be plural.

Write a sentence for each of the verbs below.

1. play _____

2. swims _____

3. walk _____

4. jump _____

5. eat _____

6. sleeps _____

7. makes _____

8. repair _____

9. glows _____

10. skips _____

Let's Make Sentences!

A **sentence** must express a clear thought. You know that a sentence must have a subject and a predicate.

There are four types of sentences: **declarative, interrogative, imperative,** and **exclamatory.** The following are definitions for each type of sentence.

> **Declarative:** makes a statement and ends with a period
> **Interrogative:** asks a question and ends with a question mark
> **Imperative:** gives a command and ends with a period
> **Exclamatory:** shows feeling and ends with an exclamation point

Write five sentences on the lines below. Draw a box around your subject. Draw a circle around the predicate.

1. _____
2. _____
3. _____
4. _____
5. _____

Now look back at the sentences that you wrote. What type of sentences are they? Write the type of sentence on each line below. For example, if sentence number one is interrogative, write interrogative on the line next to number one below.

1. _____
2. _____
3. _____
4. _____
5. _____

What Kind of Sentence?

Remember that there are four types of sentences: **declarative, interrogative, imperative,** and **exclamatory.**

Read the sentences below. Write the type of sentence next to the sentence.

1. Do not jump in the pool. _____

2. What a fantastic ride that was! _____

3. Can you sleep over at my house this Friday? _____

4. My mother is a lawyer. _____

5. Ralph went to college last fall. _____

6. Did you see Finding Nemo? _____

7. Ouch! That hurt! _____

8. Don't talk to me now. _____

9. I learned to swim when I was three. _____

10. Why did you do that? _____

Declaring Your Hobbies

Hobbies are things that we do because they interest us, and we enjoy them. For example, some of your hobbies may be painting, reading, or collecting baseball cards.

Think about your hobbies. Write at least four hobbies that you enjoy.

_____

_____

_____

_____

Now, write a **declarative** sentence about each of your hobbies.

1. _____

2. _____

3. _____

4. _____

Let's Talk About Jobs

There are lots of different jobs that people have. Some jobs are listed below. Beneath each job, write three declarative sentences about that job.

Example: **Police Officer**
The police officer drives a police car.
She helps keep people safe.
The police officer has a badge.

Doctor

_____

_____

_____

Teacher

_____

_____

_____

Construction Worker

_____

_____

_____

Dentist

_____

_____

_____

Question Me!

An interrogative sentence asks a question and ends with a question mark. Imagine that you have a pen pal who lives in a foreign country. You have no idea what life is like in that country. Write a letter to your pen pal and ask him or her all the questions that you would like answered. When you are done, go back and circle all of your interrogative sentences.

Dear _____,

_____

_____

_____

_____

_____

_____

_____

_____

_____

_____

_____

_____

_____

_____

Your pen pal,

_____

Ask a Celebrity

Imagine that you have the opportunity to interview a television or movie star. What questions would you ask? Write five interrogative sentences.

Name of Celebrity: _____

Movie or Television Show: _____

1. _____
_____

2. _____
_____

3. _____
_____

4. _____
_____

5. _____
_____

Signs, Signs

Have you ever gone on a trip and played a game in which you looked for street signs? Street signs give drivers hints about things that they should expect. Look at the street signs below. Choose five of them, and write an imperative sentence for each one. Then, draw the sign next to your sentence.

Example: Look out for deer crossing!

1. _____
   _____

2. _____
   _____

3. _____
   _____

4. _____
   _____

5. _____
   _____

85 Lesson Launchers: **Basic Grammar and Usage**
© 2010 Walch Education

A Day at the County Fair!

An **exclamatory** sentence is a sentence that shows feeling. It ends with an exclamation point.

Read the following story. Underline all of the exclamatory sentences.

A Fair Day!

One day last fall, my grandparents took me to a county fair. Have you ever been to one? This fair is really big and has lots of animals. I saw cows, goats, and sheep. I even got to pet some llamas! We went to the pulling barn and saw tractors pulling weights. We went to the small racetrack and saw horses racing. I loved the horses! After the races were over, my grandfather took me to pet the horses. They were big and very pretty.

After we visited the animals, we finally got to go on the rides. I went on the roller coaster three times! Have you ever been on a roller coaster? It was scary at first, but lots of fun. At the end of the day, we had fried dough. It was really yummy. I had a great time at the fair! I hope I get to go again next year!

Now answer the following questions.

1. How many declarative sentences are in the story? _____

2. How many interrogative sentences are there? _____

3. How many imperative sentences are there? _____

The Best Birthday Ever

Exclamatory sentences show expression, feeling, or emotion.

Examples: Happy Birthday to you!

What a great trick!

Ouch! That really hurt!

Imagine that it is your birthday. Your best friend plans a surprise birthday party and invites all your friends and family. Write a story about your birthday. You should have at least five exclamatory sentences in your story.

My Birthday Party

_____

_____

_____

_____

_____

_____

_____

_____

_____

_____

_____

Ready, Set, Complete!

An **imperative** sentence gives a command. A **declarative** sentence makes a statement. Complete each of the following sentences to fit the category. Be sure to punctuate correctly.

Imperative

1. Please _____

2. Do not _____

3. Wash _____

4. Watch out _____

5. Be careful _____

Declarative

6. My mom _____

7. Mrs. Watson _____

8. Purple _____

9. Turtles _____

10. Our home _____

Question or Command?

Complete the following sentences. Then, write **imperative** or **interrogative** to describe each sentence.

1. Why did you _____
   _____

2. Please watch _____
   _____

3. Do not _____
   _____

4. Are we _____
   _____

5. Do you _____
   _____

6. Look out for _____
   _____

7. Would you _____
   _____

8. Did Julia _____
   _____

9. Don't _____
   _____

10. Is she _____
    _____

85 Lesson Launchers: **Basic Grammar and Usage**
© 2010 Walch Education

Question or Exclamation?

An **interrogative** sentence asks a question. An **exclamatory** sentence shows feeling. Complete the following sentences to fit the category.

Interrogative

1. Why _____

2. Would you _____

3. Can _____

4. May I _____

5. Should _____

Exclamatory

6. That _____

7. What _____

8. Wow! _____

9. Great _____

10. This _____

Simple Sentences

A **sentence** has a subject and a predicate and expresses a complete thought. A **simple sentence** may have one or more subjects. It may also have one or more predicates. However, a **simple sentence** always expresses one complete thought.

Examples: The letter carrier delivered our mail. (one subject, **letter carrier**, and one predicate, **delivered**)

Judy and I walked to the store. (two subjects, **Judy, I,** and one predicate, **walked**)

The children swam and played. (one subject, **children,** and two predicates, **swam, played**)

Now, write five simple sentences.

1. _____

2. _____

3. _____

4. _____

5. _____

85 Lesson Launchers: **Basic Grammar and Usage**
© 2010 Walch Education

Combining Sentences

A **compound sentence** contains two simple sentences joined by a conjunction. The conjunctions **and, but, so, if, yet, or,** and **nor** can be used to join two simple sentences to make a compound sentence.

Examples: The astronaut trained for five years. The astronaut was very prepared for flight.

The astronaut trained for five years, **so** he was very prepared for flight. (A comma is used to separate the two simple sentences.)

Read the following sentences. Then, combine the two sentences into one compound sentence.

1. I love your hair. It is so curly!

   _____

2. That movie was fantastic. The lead actor was wonderful.

   _____

3. I wish I could go. My mother won't let me.

   _____

4. Jason cannot swim. He loves the beach.

   _____

5. She doesn't like spinach. She doesn't like broccoli.

   _____

6. Harriet went to the doctor. The doctor said she has the flu.

   _____

Compound Separation

A simple sentence is made up of one independent clause. A **compound sentence** contains two independent clauses (simple sentences) joined by a conjunction.

Read the following compound sentences. Rewrite each sentence, changing it from one compound sentence into two simple sentences.

1. Alice takes great care of herself, so she is very healthy.

   _____

2. I love to stay up late reading, but I am so tired in the morning.

   _____

3. David would love to go with us, but he cannot ski.

   _____

4. I could do that, but I need more practice.

   _____

5. We could go to the movies, or we could watch one at home.

   _____

6. He wanted to learn to fly, yet he looked so scared.

   _____

85 Lesson Launchers: **Basic Grammar and Usage**
© 2010 Walch Education

Make Them Complete!

Complete the following sentences. Each sentence should be a **simple sentence**.

1. Niagara Falls _____

2. Were the Egyptians _____

3. _____ in a hot-air balloon.

4. The stars _____

5. Astronauts _____

Complete the following sentences. Each sentence should be a **compound sentence**.

6. Mangrove trees _____

_____

7. Girl Scouts _____

_____

8. Puzzles _____

_____

9. You wanted to go _____

_____

10. The thunderstorm _____

_____

Fishing for Fragments

A **fragment** is a group of words that is used incorrectly as a sentence. A fragment is not a sentence because it is missing part of a sentence, such as a subject or a verb. It may also be a fragment simply because it is not a complete thought.

Examples: The bright red wagon. (lacks a verb)
If you drive right into town. (is not a complete thought)
Running down the street. (lacks a subject)

Choose five of the fragments below and make them into complete sentences. Don't forget to punctuate!

The tall building

The choppy ocean water   His jacket

The little mouse

over the fence   flew into the sky

Their parents

walking across the field   caught a fish

1. _____

2. _____

3. _____

4. _____

5. _____

85 Lesson Launchers: **Basic Grammar and Usage**

Run-On or Complete?

A **run-on sentence** occurs when two sentences are not separated or joined properly.

Example: I asked Mrs. Jones for lunch money she gave me some.
(Run-on sentence)
(This sentence can be joined properly in these ways:
I asked Mrs. Jones for lunch money. She gave me some.
I asked Mrs. Jones for lunch money; she gave me some.
I asked Mrs. Jones for lunch money, and she gave me some.)

Read the following sentences. If the sentence is correct, write **complete sentence** on the line. If the sentence is a run-on, write **run-on** on the line.

1. I asked you twice already I wish you would just answer me.

   _____

2. You can go; all you have to do is ask.

   _____

3. Please don't make me go I don't want to go.

   _____

4. Jake thought that the inning would never end it seemed to go on forever.

   _____

5. He said he would take us, but he hasn't shown up yet.

   _____

6. Do you really think that would be okay with your mother?

   _____

7. I have an extra ticket to the basketball game would you like to go?

   _____

8. Have you ever played marbles it is really fun.

   _____

Answer Key

PARTS OF SPEECH

Page 1: Find the Nouns
1. Lily, puddle
2. Anthony, hockey
3. Mrs. Mason, book, class
4. George Washington, president
5. United States, place
6. dad, ball
7. Casey, milk
8. John, newspaper, day
9. Sophie, stars, night
10. Australia, country

Page 2: A Proper Family Tree
Answers will vary.

Page 3: Signed, Sealed, and Delivered!
Answers will vary.

Page 4: A School of Nouns
The following should be circled:
crew, crowd, committee, family, army, constellation, team, troop, class, group, assembly

Page 5: Which Noun Is Which?
1. Circle: shampoo, flag; Square: team
2. Circle: pen; Square: crowd, colony
3. Circle: glass, hammer; Square: pair
4. Circle: paper clip; Square: crew, species
5. Circle: napkin, daisy; Square: army
6. Circle: television, hat; Square: chorus
7. Circle: basket, camera; Square: committee
8. Circle: game, ocean; Square: staff
9. Circle: pillow; Square: club, pack
10. Circle: marker, eraser; Square: band

Page 6: Make It Plural!
1. houses
2. chicks
3. foxes
4. churches
5. bushes
6. classes
7. buckets
8. couches
9. shirts
10. books
11. movies
12. buses
13. radishes
14. rockets
15. beaches
16. carrots
17. circuses
18. toothbrushes
19. shoes
20. porches

Page 7: Where Does It Go?
Singular: pizza, jacket, student, person, rabbit, seagull, turkey, flower
Plural: hats, bees, boots, pennies, clouds, houses, people, fireflies

Page 8: What Do They Possess?
Possible Answers:
2. the teacher's book 3. Sally's violin 4. the firefighter's helmet 5. the doctor's office

Page 9: What's the Action?
The following should be underlined:
1. walked
2. hit
3. read
4. pushed
5. watched
6. drank
7. swung
8. drove
9. jumped
10. picked

Page 10: Susie's Day
What a Day!
One day, Susie woke up late. She rushed out of bed. Susie threw on her clothes and brushed her hair. She ran down the stairs to eat her breakfast. After breakfast, she brushed her teeth. She waved good-bye to her mother and hurried out the door. Susie saw the bus. The bus stopped in front of her house. Susie jumped on. She greeted her friends. The bus driver drove away. Susie began her school day.

Page 11: What Are They Doing?
1. walked
2. rides
3. swims
4. jumped
5. watched
6. pounced
7. scored
8. read
9. talks
10. licked

Page 12: To Be or Not to Be?
1. is 2. is 3. are 4. is 5. is 6. is 7. are 8. is 9. is 10. is
Sentences will vary.

Page 13: A Helping of Verbs
1. should
2. was
3. will
4. has
5. may
6. shall
7–8. Answers will vary.

Page 14: Past or Present?
2. sits; present
3. sang; past
4. barks; present
5. looks; present
6. rode; past
7. float; present
8. flew; past
9. laughed; past
10. slept; past
11. swam; past
12. plays; present

Page 15: What Will Happen?
1. The bird will sing.
2. Jade will color in her coloring book.

3. John will wash his new car.
4. Our cat will meow.
5. I will hit the tennis ball.
6. Derek will sail in a little sailboat.
7. The dog will eat his food.
8. Carrie will swim in the swimming pool.

Page 16: Irregular Verbs

1. see—saw	9. shake—shook
2. am—was	10. fight—fought
3. come—came	11. choose—chose
4. eat—ate	12. fly—flew
5. freeze—froze	13. steal—stole
6. swim—swam	14. write—wrote
7. wear—wore	15. drink—drank
8. ring—rang	

Page 17: Back to the Present

1. begin	6. grow
2. blow	7. draw
3. break	8. fall
4. go	9. give
5. speak	10. ride

Page 18: One, Two, Three, or More?

1. plural	6. plural
2. singular	7. singular
3. plural	8. plural
4. plural	9. plural
5. singular	10. singular

Page 19: Make It Plural!

1. play	6. swim
2. eat	7. walk
3. sleep	8. listen
4. talk	9. look
5. write	10. grow

Page 20: Double Meanings

1. noun	6. verb
2. verb	7. noun
3. verb	8. verb
4. noun	9. verb
5. noun	10. noun

Page 21: Who Are You?
Answers will vary.

Page 22: An Indefinite Answer

1. a	6. an
2. a	7. a
3. a	8. an
4. an	9. a
5. a	10. an

Page 23: Let's Go Skiing!

Last December, Nick's family went skiing in Vail, Colorado. When they arrived at <u>the</u> ski area, Nick was very excited. He looked around at all of <u>the</u> people. They carried skis, poles, and snowboards. Nick had <u>a</u> brand-new pair of skis. He couldn't wait to try them! His sister, Kate, had <u>an</u> older snowboard that she had borrowed. She was eager to get on <u>the</u> slopes. Nick went into <u>the</u> lodge to put on his ski boots. He put on <u>a</u> heavy pair of socks. Then he put on his boots. After wrapping <u>a</u> scarf around his neck, he was ready to go! He went out into <u>the</u> cold and put on his skis. He and his father got in line at <u>the</u> chairlift. When <u>the</u> chair came around, Nick hopped on. <u>The</u> chairlift brought Nick and his father all <u>the</u> way to <u>the</u> top of <u>the</u> mountain. They got off of <u>the</u> chairlift and waited for Kate and Mom. When all four of them were at <u>the</u> top, they pulled down their goggles. Nick skied down <u>the</u> mountain. It was <u>a</u> great day!

Page 24: You Choose an Adverb!
Possible answers:

1. quickly	6. noisily
2. easily	7. slowly
3. gently	8. angrily
4. loudly	9. hard
5. fast	10. very

Page 25: Adverbs Versus Adjectives

1. adverb ❯ talk	9. adjective ❯ octopus
2. adverb ❯ flew	10. adjective ❯ grass
3. adverb ❯ well	11. adjective ❯ sea
4. adjective ❯ play	12. adjective ❯ movies
5. adverb ❯ walk	13. adverb ❯ quietly
6. adjective ❯ water	14. adjective ❯ player
7. adverb ❯ old	15. adverb ❯ squeeze
8. adjective ❯ people	

Page 26: Substitute Pronouns

1. It	6. they
2. we	7. them
3. they	8. them
4. He	9. they
5. She	10. it

Page 27: Pronoun Possession

1. Our	9. Your
2. mine	10. their
3. their	11. his
4. her	12. its
5. their	13. its
6. her	14. our
7. mine	15. his
8. our	

Page 28: Name That Conjunction!

1. Neither, nor
2. both, and
3. either, or
4. whether, or
5. both, and
6. Neither, nor
7. Whether, or
8. Both, and

Page 29: Please Don't Interject!

1. Wow!
2. Jeepers!
3. Ouch!
4. no interjection
5. Cool!
6. Oops!
7. Uh-oh!
8. Help!
9. Gosh!
10. Oh my goodness!
11. Sweet!
12. no interjection

Page 30: Test Your Noun Skills

Common—uncle, computer, water
Proper—London, California, Abraham Lincoln

On Tuesday, children from our school went to a wild animal park. The children on the soccer <u>team</u> went. The students from the school <u>orchestra</u> went. The boys and girls from the after-school <u>club</u> went. My <u>family</u> helped out on the trip, and they went, too. We saw a <u>flock</u> of birds. We saw a <u>school</u> of fish. We saw a <u>pod</u> of seals. We saw a <u>herd</u> of elephants and a <u>pack</u> of wolves. We even saw an <u>army</u> of ants at our picnic.

1. pennies
2. apples
3. beaches
4. cities
5. him, her, you, them, or it
6. your
7. my, your, his, or her
8. their

Page 31: Show What You Know!

I love to go to <u>the</u> zoo. My <u>favorite</u> animals are <u>the</u> giraffes. They are so <u>neat</u> with their <u>long, skinny</u> necks and their spots. I think it would be really <u>cool</u> to be able to reach my head way up into trees <u>the</u> way giraffes can. I also love <u>the</u> polar bears. They are so <u>big</u> and <u>furry</u>. I wonder if they are as <u>soft</u> and <u>cuddly</u> as they look!

1. adjective
2. adverb
3. adjective
4. adjective
5. adjective
6. adverb
7. adjective
8. adverb

CAPITALIZATION

Page 32: Luck o' the Irish
Errors are underlined.

A Green Day!

Every <u>m</u>arch my family gathers together. <u>b</u>ecause we are a large <u>i</u>rish family, March 17 is a very special <u>D</u>ay for us. <u>w</u>hy? <u>i</u>t is special because <u>m</u>arch 17 is <u>st</u>. <u>p</u>atrick's <u>d</u>ay! <u>o</u>ur family dresses in green <u>C</u>lothing and dances to Irish music.

<u>m</u>y little cousin, <u>b</u>ridget, performs <u>i</u>rish step dancing for us. <u>m</u>y <u>a</u>unt <u>c</u>olleen makes <u>C</u>orned <u>B</u>eef and cabbage. <u>m</u>y mother even makes green mashed potatoes! My <u>u</u>ncle Reilly makes <u>i</u>rish soda bread, an <u>i</u>rish tradition. <u>s</u>omeday I hope to go to <u>i</u>reland and celebrate <u>st</u>. <u>p</u>atrick's <u>d</u>ay there!

Page 33: Holidays Around the Year
Answers will vary.

Page 34: Where in the World?

1. England
2. Missouri
3. Colorado
4. California
5. France
6. Washington
7. Spain
8. Hawaii
9. Canada
10. Texas
11. Utah
12. Maryland

Page 35: Let's Talk About You
Answers will vary.

Page 36: A Capital Letter

423 <u>p</u>alm <u>s</u>treet
Sanibel <u>i</u>sland, <u>f</u>lorida 95860
<u>a</u>ugust 22, 2003

Ms. <u>g</u>ail Scott
2986 <u>w</u>alker <u>b</u>oulevard
Suite 46
Littleton, <u>c</u>olorado 80128

Dear <u>m</u>s. Scott,

<u>t</u>hank you for your interest in my puppies. I have been caring for golden retrievers since <u>m</u>ay of 1998. The puppies will be available in <u>d</u>ecember, so you will have your puppy in time for <u>c</u>hristmas. I am happy to reserve one of <u>r</u>usty's puppies for you.

<u>w</u>ill you be flying from <u>l</u>ittleton to <u>s</u>anibel <u>i</u>sland? It would be best if you could fly into the <u>f</u>ort <u>m</u>yers <u>a</u>irport. Arriving on a <u>m</u>onday or <u>t</u>hursday would be best. Could you let me know your plans by <u>s</u>eptember 30?

<u>i</u> will look forward to hearing from you soon.

sincerely,
Pauline Roy
<u>p</u>auline <u>r</u>oy

Page 37: Capital Review
The following should be circled: New York, Wednesday, Labor Day, Arkansas, Amsterdam, Mount Ranier, December, Yellowstone National Park, Wal-Mart, Statue of Liberty, Independence Day, February, Monday. Water, rocks, puppy, and refrigerator should not be capitalized.

PUNCTUATION

Page 38: Period Practice Makes Perfect!
1. Mister – Mr.
2. United States – U.S.
3. Reverend – Rev.
4. Kelly Colleen – K.C.
5. Park Avenue – Park Ave.
6. 100 feet – 100 ft.
7. Franklin Delano Roosevelt – F.D.R.
8. Monday – Mon.
9. December – Dec.
10. Richard, Junior – Richard, Jr.

Page 39: Excuse Me, Mr. President
Answers will vary.

Page 40: Choose the Punctuation
Answers will vary.

Page 41: A Letter to Grandma
Dear Grandma,
   How are you [?] I am doing really well [.]
   Next week is my last week of school [.]
I am so excited [!] Mom and Dad have lots of fun things
planned for the summer [.] We are going to a water park
and to the zoo [.] I can't wait to see all of the animals [!]
Mom even said that I can bring a friend with me [.]
   Are you going to come and visit soon [?] I hope so [!] I
really miss you so much and can't wait to see you [.]
              Lots of love,
              Abby

Page 42: It All Ends Here
1. My school has 400 students [.]
2. How many students go to your school [?]
3. Do you like music [?]
4. My teacher is great [!]
5. Ouch! That hurt [!]
6. Are you okay [?]
7. My mom works in a hospital [.]
8. Do you have a brother or a sister [?]
9. That's wonderful [!]
10. Do you want to visit our school [?]

Page 43: Using Commas
Answers will vary.

Page 44: When I Grow Up . . .
Possible answers:
1. Well, I would like to be a teacher.
2. Yes, my job would be inside.
3. No, I would not work on a farm.
4. No, I would not have my own office.
5. Well, I don't know.
6. No, I would not be boss.
7. Yes, I would have fun teaching children.

Page 45: Comma Madness
Commas are in bold.
1. Please, Veronica, don't walk in the mud!
2. Aaron looks very sad today. (✔)
3. Emily, why don't you come to the movies with us?
4. Mr. Moore, may I go to the library?
5. Pete Sampras is a great tennis player. (✔)
6. George Washington was our first president. (✔)
7. Mom, may I go out and play?
8. How do you get to Hawaii, Uncle Harry?
9. I wonder, Mrs. Mowatt, if I can take that book home with me.
10. Jamie, let's go swimming!

Page 46: Set It Off!
Answers will vary.

Page 47: Red Letter Days
Commas are in bold.
1. On November 3, 1998, we got our first snow of the year.
2. We adopted our cat on March 26, 1995.
3. On May 6, 2001, my family went to our family reunion.
4. My cousin was born on October 17, 2003.
5. July 4, 2000, was a great Independence Day!
6. On December 23, 2001, we had a huge snowstorm!
7. Aisha's sister was born on January 1, 2003, New Year's Day!
8. On October 3, 1997, Karen and Paul got married.
9–10. Sentences will vary.

Page 48: Around the World
Commas are in bold.
1. Julia lives in San Francisco, California.
2. Big Ben is in London, England.
3. Paul's aunt visits us in Boulder, Colorado every summer.
4. Our family vacations in Bar Harbor, Maine.
5. The Grand Tetons are in Jackson, Wyoming.
6. The cruise ship stopped at Cancun, Mexico.
7. I love to visit Montreal, Canada.
8. My brother lives in Portland, Oregon.
9. Every year we go skiing in Vail, Colorado.
10. Mardi Gras is very exciting in New Orleans, Louisiana.

Page 49: Where Have You Been?
Answers will vary.

Page 50: Compound Commas

Commas are in bold.

1. You said you wanted to go ice-skating, yet you don't know how to skate!
2. My mother reminds me to wear a helmet, but I always remember anyway.
3. I asked him to a movie, and he said that he would go.
4. Do you want to go swimming, or would you rather build a sand castle?
5. Mrs. Johnson said I could pick the flowers, but they had already died.
6. The mall was closed, so we went out to dinner instead.
7. Lily asked for a video game, and her dad said she could get one.
8. I'd like you to go with us, but you said that you were not interested.

Page 51: Comma Camp

Commas are in bold.

Dear Mom and Dad,

   How are you? I am doing really well. I love being at camp. There are so many fun activities to do. My favorites are sailing, soccer, and pottery class. I am becoming a very good sailor! Dad, wait until you see how much I know about sailing! I really like it. Soccer is also lots of fun. My counselor took us to a professional soccer game last Friday. We drove to Manchester, New Hampshire, and watched the game in a big stadium. It was really cool! I am also enjoying pottery. Can you believe it? Yes, I am actually quite good! Mom, I made you a really neat bowl. I can't wait to give it to you. The kids in my cabin are really nice, too. Michael, the youngest one of us, is also from Boston. He lives close to where we live.

   Well, I should get going. It is almost time for dinner. I hope you are doing well. See you soon!

                                    Love,
                                    Brian

Page 52: My Prized Possessions

Sentences will vary but should contain the following:

2. the boy's shoe
3. Mom's car
4. Amy's baseball glove
5. Julia and Michelle's sister
6. the teacher's watch

Page 53: What Do They Possess?

Answers are in bold.

1. John's baseball glove is old and worn out.
2. The boats' masts are very tall.
3. The house's shutters are painted green.
4. The team's banner is brand-new.
5. A sunflower's petals are yellow.
6. The roller coaster's track was really curvy.
7. Vermont's "claim to fame" is Ben and Jerry's ice cream.
8. The swans' necks are very graceful.
9. The group's colors are green and gold.
10. Jess's scarf was pink and white.

Page 54: Contraction Action

1. you + are
2. he + is
3. we + are
4. it + is
5. did + not
6. you + will
7. could + not
8. he + will
9. we + will
10. they + are

Page 55: Don't Quote Me!

3. "Great! We had a spelling bee and I won," Jamie replied.
4. "You did? That is great," said her mom.
5. Jamie said, "I got a blue ribbon for winning." (correct)
6. "Let's put it on the refrigerator," said her mom.
7. Then her mom said, "We'll show Dad when he gets home."
8. "Then we will both be so proud of you," said her mom. (correct)
9. Jamie said, "Thanks, Mom."
10. In a shy voice, Jamie said, "I am proud, too!" (correct)

Page 56 Quotation Marks or Underline?

1. <u>Highlights Magazine</u>
2. <u>Where the Sidewalk Ends</u>
3. <u>The Rescuers Down Under</u>
4. <u>The New York Times</u>
5. <u>Finding Nemo</u>
6. "Amelia Earhart"
7. <u>Sports Illustrated for Kids</u>
8. "Two Friends"
9. <u>Lewis and Clark</u>
10. "Animal Crackers"
11. "The Swing"
12. "Aro the Crow"

Page 57: Explaining Parentheses

Answers will vary.

Page 58: Choose Your Parentheses

Sentences will vary.

SUBJECTS AND PREDICATES

Page 59: Subject Search
1. aunt
2. cat
3. pavement
4. umbrella
5. phone

6–10. Sentences will vary.

Page 60: Insert a Subject
Possible answers:
1. frog
2. cat
3. Florida
4. Birds
5. Hammocks
6. roof
7. Red
8. Chipmunks
9. Thunder
10. Dogs

Page 61: Perfect Predicates
1. The fish <u>has blue and green stripes</u>.
2. The flowers <u>are very pretty</u>.
3. Akira <u>went skiing last winter</u>.
4. Matthew <u>plays hockey every Monday night</u>.
5. Fiona <u>is the best pitcher on our softball team</u>.
6. All the leaves <u>fell off the tree</u>.
7. Danny <u>rode his bike to the boardwalk</u>.
8. The house <u>has green shutters.</u>
9. The beach <u>is covered with pretty seashells</u>.
10. Disney World <u>is home to Mickey and Minnie Mouse</u>.

Page 62: Who Is Your Hero?
Answers will vary.

Page 63: Add a Complement
Complements are underlined:
1. hopped <u>through our backyard</u>.
2. plays <u>on the lacrosse team</u>.
3. watches <u>the news every night</u>.
4. is <u>slower than the rabbit</u>.
5. don't <u>belong in the house</u>.
6. loves <u>to eat watermelon</u>.
7. cried <u>when she woke up</u>.
8. has <u>four legs</u>.
9. dribble <u>the ball really well</u>.
10. is <u>a great place to sail a boat</u>.

Sentences may vary.

Page 64: Finding the Right Complement
1. The crowd yelled when the player scored.
2. The pilot flew to Chicago every week.
3. The sprinkler helps to water the garden.
4. Stuart looked very tired.
5. The castle was made entirely of stone.
6. Breakfast is my favorite meal of the day.

Page 65: Subject and Predicate Review
1. dictionary
2. Lemonade
3. Mrs. Knowles
4. Boston Celtics
5. I

6–15. Sentences will vary.
16. more slowly than I do
17. in a barn behind our house
18. to smoke
19. scary
20. really nice

Page 66: Hawaiian Agreement
1. is
2. are
3. has
4. has
5. have
6. picks
7. look, see
8. sees
9. are
10. hurt, hurt

Page 67: Don't You Agree?
Possible answers:
1. We <u>play</u> well.
2. She <u>swims</u> each day.
3. Jane and Jim <u>walk</u> to school.
4. The girls <u>jump</u> rope.
5. You can <u>eat</u> with us.
6. The cat <u>sleeps</u> many hours.
7. Mom <u>makes</u> good pancakes.
8. I will <u>repair</u> the bike.
9. The sign <u>glows</u> in the dark.
10. Peter <u>skips</u> rocks at the pond.

SENTENCES

Page 68: Let's Make Sentences!
Possible answers:
1. I have done my drawing.
2. Have you done yours?
3. Well, do it now.
4. It took you ten minutes to finish it.
5. I think it looks great!
1. declarative
2. interrogative
3. imperative
4. declarative
5. exclamatory

Page 69: What Kind of Sentence?
1. imperative
2. exclamatory
3. interrogative
4. declarative
5. declarative
6. interrogative
7. exclamatory
8. imperative
9. declarative
10. interrogative

Page 70: Declaring Your Hobbies
Answers will vary.

Page 71: Let's Talk About Jobs
Answers will vary.

Page 72: Question Me!
Answers will vary.

Page 73: Ask a Celebrity
Answers will vary.

Page 74: Street Signs
Answers will vary.

Page 75: A Day at the County Fair!

A Fair Day!

One day last fall, my grandparents took me to a county fair. Have you ever been to one? This fair is really big and has lots of animals. I saw cows, goats, and sheep. <u>I even got to pet some llamas!</u> We went to the pulling barn and saw tractors pulling weights. We went to the small racetrack and saw horses racing. <u>I loved the horses!</u> After the races were over, my grandfather took me to pet the horses. They were big and very pretty.

After we visited the animals, we finally got to go on the rides. <u>I went on the roller coaster three times!</u> Have you ever been on a roller coaster? It was scary at first, but lots of fun. At the end of the day, we had fried dough. It was really yummy. <u>I had a great time at the fair! I hope I get to go again next year!</u>

1. 11
2. 2
3. 0

Page 76: The Best Birthday Ever
Answers will vary.

Page 77: Ready, Set, Complete!
Possible answers:

Imperative
1. Please stop crying.
2. Do not run with scissors.
3. Wash behind your ears.
4. Watch out for mosquitos.
5. Be careful when using sharp tools.

Declarative
6. My mom is a lawyer.
7. Mrs. Watson is our neighbor.
8. Purple is not my favorite color.
9. Turtles have hard shells.
10. Our home is very comfortable.

Page 78: Question or Command?
Possible answers:

1. Why did you tell our secret? interrogative
2. Please watch your step. imperative
3. Do not shout. imperative
4. Are we going? interrogative
5. Do you know the answer? interrogative
6. Look out for falling rocks. imperative
7. Would you know the time? interrogative
8. Did Julia go to the museum? interrogative
9. Don't be late. imperative
10. Is she your cousin? interrogative

Page 79: Question or Exclamation?
Possible answers:

Interrogative:
1. Why did you go without asking?
2. Would you like to see my cat?
3. Can pigs fly?
4. May I study with you?
5. Should we go together?

Exclamatory:
6. That was great fun!
7. What a beautiful sky!
8. Wow! He sure ran fast!
9. Great job on that report!
10. This is wonderful!

Page 80: Simple Sentences
Answers will vary.

Page 81: Combining Sentences
Answers will vary.

Page 82: Compound Separation
1. Alice takes great care of herself. She is very healthy.
2. I love to stay up late reading. I am so tired in the morning.
3. David would love to go with us. He cannot ski.
4. I could do that. I need more practice.
5. We could go to the movies. We could watch one at home.
6. He wanted to learn to fly. He looked so scared.

Page 83: Make Them Complete!
Answers will vary.

Page 84: Fishing for Fragments
Answers will vary.

Page 85: Run-On or Complete?
1. run-on
2. complete sentence
3. run-on
4. run-on
5. complete sentence
6. complete sentence
7. run-on
8. run-on

WALCH EDUCATION®

extending and enhancing learning

Let's stay in touch!

Thank you for purchasing these Walch Education materials. Now, we'd like to support you in your role as an educator. **Register now** and we'll provide you with updates on related publications, online resources, and more. You can register online at www.walch.com/newsletter, or fill out this form and fax or mail it to us.

Name _____ Date _____

School name _____

School address_____

City _____ State _____ Zip _____

Phone number (home) _____ (school) _____

E-mail _____

Grade level(s) taught _____ Subject area(s) _____

Where did you purchase this publication? _____

When do you primarily purchase supplemental materials? _____

What moneys were used to purchase this publication?

[   ] School supplemental budget

[   ] Federal/state funding

[   ] Personal

[   ] Please sign me up for Walch Education's free quarterly e-newsletter, *Education Connection.*

[   ] Please notify me regarding free *Teachable Moments* downloads.

[   ] Yes, you may use my comments in upcoming communications.

COMMENTS _____

_____

_____

_____

Please FAX this completed form to 888-991-5755, or mail it to:
Customer Service, Walch Education, 40 Walch Drive, Portland, ME 04103

85 Lesson Launchers: **Basic Grammar and Usage**
© 2010 Walch Education